CONTAINER GARDENING

CONTAINER GARDENING

Ethne Clarke

WITH A FOREWORD BY
MAX DAVIDSON

This edition first published in 1996 by the
Promotional Reprint Company, Ltd,
Deacon House,
65 Old Church Street,
London SW3 5BS
exclusively for Chapters in Canada
and Chris Beckett Ltd in New Zealand.

Text © Ethne Clarke 1996
Design and layout © The Promotional Reprint Company, Ltd 1996
Photography © Garden Picture Library 1996

ISBN 1 85648 295 2

Publishing Manager *Casey Horton*
Editor *Jennifer Spaeth*
Designer *Ming Cheung*

Publisher's Note
Readers should note that plant breeders introduce new cultivars all the time.
Please check your seed catalogues for the latest ones.

> **WARNING**
> If using chemical herbicides,
> fungicides or insecticides, be sure to
> follow exactly the manufacturer's
> instructions

Printed and bound in Hong Kong

CONTENTS

FOREWORD

When we look back at the history of gardening, we can imagine that most gardening was done in containers, from the Hanging Gardens of Babylon to large urns, perhaps on pedestals, which might have decorated the gardens of Roman and Greek villas.

It was not until the late Middle Ages, when gardening began to move away from simply growing vegetables in cultivated ground, that flowers began to take up the importance they have assumed today.

Yet fashions continually change, even in gardening, and, at present, containers are very much in vogue to provide colour in gardens, large and small. The beauty of hanging baskets and window boxes is that they provide something at eye-level to admire.

What more delightful welcome can there be to a home than to see a basket full of trailing fuchsias or a half-barrel by the front door full of bright scarlet geraniums or a dazzling array of petunias?

Tubs and urns are perfect for providing flowers and foliage on patios and terraces. In small, low-maintenance gardens, which are usually planted with trees, shrubs and perennials, containers can provide seasonal colour with a host of different annuals in summer and biennials, such as pansies, in winter.

It was once imagined that containers were simply for growing an ever-changing display of annual plants. Yet they can be used equally well, if not better, for perennials, alpines, shrubs and even small trees.

Containers can be used to grow many of the plants you would find in a conventional garden, even down to soft fruits such as strawberries, leaf vegetables and, of course, herbs.

There is a huge range of containers you can get nowadays, from the inexpensive growing bags for vegetables to terracotta, stone, wood, plastic and concrete tubs. You can even have those wonderful Oriental glazed containers, which will sit just as happily on a patio as in a conservatory. You do not need to spend a fortune. Some plastic is made to imitate expensive lead containers without the weight, and reconstituted stone can look as good as the real thing once it has the patina of age on it.

Urns on stone pedestals can easily provide a wonderful focal point in the garden by adding a note of formality and grandeur to a classic garden design scheme.

Modern, lightweight composts mean that urns and planters on patios, terraces and balconies can be moved around as necessary and are no longer the almost permanent fixtures (unless emptied) they once were in days gone by.

Feeding, too, has become easier with the advent of slow-release fertilisers, which only need to be added once a year.

If you have been put off having containers because of the need to water them frequently, you can have a micro-irrigation system connected to the tap via a simple battery-powered computer, which will care for your plants while you are away at work or on holiday.

So take a look at your garden and decide how it could be improved with a few containers.

MAX DAVIDSON

INTRODUCTION

No matter what size garden you have, there will always be room for a container or two. For town gardeners restricted to a paved terrace by the door, a few pots, urns, window boxes and so on will provide or even increase the available gardening area. Gardeners with plenty of space, however, will welcome the chance to grow special plants out of the hurly-burly of the border. Containers also provide a place to grow tender exotics in the open garden, since you can move the plants to shelter if the need arises.

Is your soil not suitable for growing as wide a range of plants as you might wish? Use containers to create mini-habitats. Need something to make a focal point in a garden plan? Try a luxuriantly planted urn. Need to cheer up a dreary entrance way? A collection of colourful flowers, grown to perfection, will present a most pleasing prospect.

In short, the versatility of container gardening will greatly expand your gardening experience.

Most plants will grow in containers and some positively benefit from the extra attention a container garden requires, but those to be avoided are ones which would, in any case, look inappropriate. So aim to have plants that are naturally reserved in their habit of growth, such as a small Japanese cutleaf maple rather than the equally colourful, but tall-growing *Acer palmatum*; compact-growing roses like the Damask 'Rose de Rescht', rather than the gorgeous Bourbon rose 'Madame Isaac Pereire'. Most perennials will do well in containers and herbs of all kinds are great favourites for container gardens (although they do benefit from being replanted every year or else pruned very hard, both roots and top growth, to keep the more ebullient plants in check).

CONTAINER BASICS

NOW THAT YOU HAVE BEEN introduced to the wonders of container gardening we will now go through the basics, which include choosing the type of container you want for your garden to the actual preparation of these containers for planting and, finally, selecting the right plant for each type of container.

Types of Containers

<u>WINDOW BOXES</u>

Window boxes are probably the most commonly used container and are available ready-made in moulded plastic, terracotta, cast concrete and wood. Choose one that is appropriate to the style of your house and, if you intend to have a box on each windowsill, do be sure they are all the same, as continuity is one of the keys to success in window box container gardening.

ABOVE: Winter colour at windowsill level is provided by bold ornamental cabbages and dainty erica, backed by an evergreen foliage display from dwarf conifers and trailing ivy.

RIGHT: Traditional flowering window box displays most often contain a collection of summer-flowering annuals, such as honey-scented petunias.

You will want the box to fit onto the windowsill comfortably; it should not overhang the edge, but be at least 2.5 cm/1 in shallower than the depth of the sill. The minimum depth for the box is 20 cm/8 in, any less and there will not be sufficient room for good root development.

Safety is a major consideration when arranging window box displays; they must be securely moored, particularly if the boxes are on upper-storey windows. All windowsills angle forward so that rain water will not collect, so you will have to wedge the front edge of the box to be sure it is level.

If you are fixing boxes below a windowsill (which you will have to if you have casement windows) use L-shaped shelving brackets to attach the box to the wall. Use this method also to secure boxes either within or below upper-storey windowsills.

Some window boxes come with 'built-in' drip trays; these are advisable for overhead boxes since it avoids the possibility of drenching anyone who maybe walking below at watering time. Boxes that are sitting on windowsills benefit from being placed on drip trays; a layer of gravel spread on the tray will prevent the bottom of the box from standing in water and it will also create a slightly humid micro-climate around the plants, which will benefit their growth.

RIGHT: Stone troughs and sinks are highly prized for containing collections of dwarf ornamental flowers and shrubs as well as alpine plants.

URNS, TUBS AND OTHER LARGE CONTAINERS

Just like window boxes, these containers are available in a wide range of materials and styles to suit every mood of garden. Large terracotta urns in the style of the classic Italian *tondo* are enormously popular for formal garden displays, as are the wooden Versailles cases. Half-barrels, cut from oak whiskey casks, offer a large growing space in which to create gardens in miniature. There are also cast concrete urns in all sorts of baroque shapes to suggest a stately home style or in simple geometric shapes for the modernists among us. Discarded enamel sinks, dressed up to look like stone sinks, had a huge popularity, but now the enamel variety are becoming as scarce as the authentic stone variety.

Whatever you choose, be sure that it has adequate drainage holes; the larger the surface area of the base, the more holes it should have. In the case of wooden half-barrels, you will probably have to drill the holes yourself; make the holes about 15 mm (½ in) in diameter, and about 15-20 cm/ 6-8 in apart, evenly spaced around the base.

Be sure you know where you mean the tubs to stay, because once they are full of compost and planted they become immovable objects. It is a good idea to put them out in place and try to envisage what the final appearance will be. Also consider the aspect – is the site in full sun, part shade or deep shade? That will have a determining effect on what you finally plant.

Because of their size, urns and barrels usually have a permanent planting feature. Stylistically, if you are using one of the more traditional shapes a standard bay or box topiary looks well, otherwise dwarf conifers, specimen evergreen shrubs, such as a dwarf rhododendron or other decorative subjects make good features for a less formal impression. But don't be hidebound by too many rules; this type of gardening invites you to be creative and adventurous.

Using evergreen shrubs or small trees not only provides year-round interest, but avoids the dead look that deciduous plants would lend towards a container garden during autumn and winter.

LEFT: A terrace is not fully furnished without a lively, varied display of containers.

Preparing for Planting

WOODEN BARRELS

Depending on the material from which they are made, the containers will require some initial preparation. Before purchasing the casks, check that the staves are sound and the hoops intact and that the assemblage is not loose; if the hoops slip it will be very difficult to get them securely back into place. The longer the barrels are empty, the drier the wood becomes and as it dries it shrinks; this is when the hoops begin to slip. Once you have the barrels home, you can hammer in a few nails below the hoops to hold them in place. Fill the barrel with water to swell the staves and thereby take up any slack. This will also leach some of the residual alcohol from the wood.

ABOVE: Summer annuals make a striking floral statement.

Wooden casks will already be partially prepared, in as much as the interior will have been charred as a preservative treatment to make it waterproof (whiskey-proof, actually). Finally, you will need to drill the necessary drainage holes.

It is a good idea to paint the barrel with a wood preservative; this is especially true of the base. Use a colourless compound, or stain with a dark tint against which the flowers will show up nicely. Some gardeners like to paint the barrels either white or green, leaving the hoops black. But once painted, it will eventually require repainting, so it is a bit of a make-work detail.

Barrels and urns should always be raised off the ground; it helps drainage and prevents earthworms, ants and other pests from colonising in the soil. I find that the best system is to stand the container on three bricks, evenly spaced around the circumference of the container. Even better are the little terracotta feet, which can be purchased at garden centres, but these are rather delicate for a substantial wooden cask.

ABOVE: A half-barrel display.

BELOW: An urn and pedestal make a classic garden display.

VERSAILLES CASES

These can be homemade or purchased ready-to-use, treated and painted and often come supplied with a metal liner in which the plants are placed. They are also sometimes fitted with casters, so the planted case can be wheeled around the terrace, but the thought of travelling containers is faintly silly and the possibility for back strain obvious. Better to decide where the container goes and leave it there.

TERRACOTTA AND CLAY

Of all the containers available, this material offers the widest range of shapes and sizes – from simple flowerpots to the elaborate, pocketed strawberry pots. There are glazed and unglazed terracotta pots and highly decorated clay pots from Malaysia and other Far East countries that are colourfully glazed and decorated with distinctly Oriental design motifs. These pots look especially good planted with grasses or bold foliage plants as flowers tend to compete with the decoration on this sort of pot.

These sorts of containers should also be raised off the ground and are what the little terracotta feet were designed for. You can also stand the

RIGHT: Changes in level on
terraces and decks can be
emphasised by a well-balanced
selection of containers chosen
to enhance the garden plan; in
this case, a formal York stone
terrace is embellished with
standard shrubs and various
flowering ornamentals.

BELOW: Formality can be
enlivened by whimsy and a coat
of colourful paint can transform
plain terracotta flowerpots and
battered watering cans into
scene-stealing props in the
garden theatre.

pots in dishes, spread with a thin layer of gravel, which will hold their feet
out of any water that collects. In time, unglazed terracotta will develop a
patina of algae. On pots that have a high relief decoration this will
enhance the motifs, but on a simple flowerpot an accumulation of green
slime just looks messy, so you may want to wash the exterior of the pots
each year at the start of the planting season. Don't scrub them clean, but
just enough to remove the worst of the accretions.

CAST CONCRETE AND OTHER MATERIALS.

This is an increasingly popular material
for all sorts of garden ornaments – from
gnomes and statues to urns and columns
of heroic scale. The quality spread is just
as broad; at the top end you have
concrete urns, which are indistinguish-
able from the finest carved stone, to
lumpen containers cast in rubber
moulds and tinted a curiously unnatural
shade of blue-grey. Since a large
container is likely to be a permanent
feature in the garden, it is worth spending as much as you can afford to obtain
a well-made and attractive product.

Just as terracotta attracts algae, these ornaments (unless given some protective coating) will eventually become colonised by lichen and moss. This, however, is to be encouraged, since it really does add to the general appearance. You can wait for this to happen at its own pace or help the process along by painting the surface of the urn with diluted yoghurt to which some peat or spent mushroom compost has been added. This provides a perfect growing medium and the urn will acquire a tapestry mantle of a soft greeny-grey and faded yellow in no time. However, do be sure you have enough mixture; a friend of mine had only enough to do half a statue of 'Diana', and she never did get around to finishing the remaining half – it really is obvious where she ran out of yoghurt.

As I mentioned earlier, stone sinks are great favourites with container gardeners, but the genuine article is hard to come by. However, old enamel sinks can still be found, although they too are becoming rare and consequently expensive. If you do find one, it can be transformed into a simulated stone sink by coating it in hypertufa mix. It is a messy job and requires patience, but the finished effect is wonderful.

BELOW: Antique lead cisterns are valuable garden ornaments and deserve special attention. Lavishly planted with convolvulus, heliotrope and annual lotus it has all the splendour of a 17th century Dutch 'flower piece' painting.

RIGHT: Genuine stone sinks and troughs are hard to come by and expensive when you do find them. But hypertufa stone sinks are easy to make using the simple recipe given here.

BELOW: A series of simple plastic urns planted with a single variety of pelargonium provide a dramatic entrance on this garden stairway.

MAKING A HYPERTUFA SINK

Assemble one plastic bucket, a garden hand fork, ready-mix cement, peat, sand and a tub of general purpose contact adhesive, such as Unibond.

Clean the sink, taking care to remove any trace of grease, dirt or scum and stand it on bricks to raise it off the ground.

Paint on a layer of adhesive all over the exterior and over the top edge into the interior by about 10 cm/4 in. Apply it evenly, but thickly. Then scumble the surface with the garden hand fork.

While the glue begins to set, thoroughly mix together one part cement with one and a half parts peat and two parts sand. Then add just enough water to make a stiff, doughy paste. This is the hypertufa mixture.

Test the surface of the glue; when it feels tacky put on a pair of rubber gloves, take a handful of hypertufa and apply it to the sink. Apply an initial layer about 15 mm/½ in thick. It should be quite rough. Work from the bottom up, taking the mix over the edge into the interior of the sink. Then, when it is filled with soil, there will not be any white enamel showing to give the game away.

Let the sink dry for a few days, then move it into position. To help it acquire the patina of age, paint it over with plain yoghurt as described above. Alternatively, you can purchase a liquid ageing compound, specially blended for the job.

Another favourite type of container, beyond the reach of most gardeners pocketbooks, is the lead cistern, embossed with a grand coat of arms and suitably impressive date – 16-something, usually. You see these cisterns for sale in auction houses at prices to make your eyes water. Fortunately, fibre-glass technology has made it possible for even the most modest garden to possess a window box or other container designed and coloured to resemble lead.

LEFT: Victorian gardeners loved fancy wirework planters such as this and filled them to overflowing with their favourite exotic plants. Replicas of these containers are widely available; use them to lend a period feel to your garden display.

Plastic pots and urns are quite common and popular nowadays, white and terracotta being the favourite colours. In fact, some of the terracotta tubs have been given a matte surface, so that from a distance you can be fooled. Unfortunately, plastic will never acquire the subtle fading and grime of ageing clay, and will always look a little too new.

These are aesthetic considerations, however, and both plastic and fibreglass do have an advantage over natural material, such as clay, for holding water better. Clay is porous, so water in the soil evaporates more quickly, which means you have to water more often, sometimes every day. So plastic can cut down on the gardening chores.

Special Feature Containers

All the containers discussed previously allow you the scope to garden as you would ordinarily. The following containers I regard as allowing you to do something special and, because of their nature, require a different approach to gardening.

BASKETS

Next to window boxes, hanging baskets are probably the most widely used container and they do deserve their popularity. Like boxes, baskets allow you to garden even if you don't have a square inch of garden to call your own and, like boxes, some pretty spectacular effects can be created by an imaginative use of foliage and flower colour. Because baskets can be ranged at any level, it is possible to create a garden display from top to toe along a house front. Their only real drawback, unfortunately, is the amount of maintenance required to keep them looking tiptop.

Wire baskets are the choice of traditionalists and they do allow greater scope in planting effects than other sorts of baskets. You can plant all around the sides and on the top to create an all over hanging garden. Wire baskets usually come in plastic covered mesh, although it is possible to find baskets made from iron lattice that look rather like a very heavy gauge umbrella skeleton. Because of their strength, such baskets come in large sizes and can be permanently planted with some weird and wonderful hanging plants. A friend of mine has transformed his basket into a pendant fernery – a stunning and surprising garden feature.

But even when it comes to wire baskets it pays to think big and to obtain the largest basket you can. The 5 cm/2 in difference in size between a 30 cm/12 in and 35 cm/14 in basket gives the larger basket 50 per cent more soil capacity, which equals greater growing capacity.

BELOW: **Don't stop at ground and windowsill level – let your garden climb the walls by using hanging baskets.**

Plastic baskets look like big salad bowls and come complete with a drip saucer attached to the base; this acts as a reservoir (although rather shallow), which can help to alleviate the intensive watering baskets require. These baskets come in various tints of green, brown, white and black and, while serviceable, lack the old-fashioned appeal of a wire basket.

Wicker baskets are one other type of basket you can use and are usually found lurking in the dark recesses of cupboards and lofts in various stages of decay. Most gardeners are loathe to throw anything away since it might come in handy some day; broken-handled, fractured-weave and split-bottomed baskets all come under that category. I can think of no better way to send them out in a blaze of glory than to plant them up, as you might a wire basket, and set them about the garden or terrace. Wicker baskets will probably endure the wet and compost for only one season, but will make a pretty show before they expire.

BELOW: Ivy and begonias find it an easy job to fill these boots – a real eyecatcher.

HOUSEHOLD ITEMS

Chimney pots, old coalscuttles, old crockery washbowls, chamber pots, wooden wine cases and old tyres (which has almost become folk art) can all be transformed into containers. I have even seen a pair of battered and tattered Doc Martens planted prettily with petunias. The danger with this type of post-modern container is that their appearance may detract from the beauty of the flowers, so use such things with a fair degree of discretion.

GROWING BAGS

Growing bags are a sort of ready-filled container that are geared to vegetable production rather than flower display. There are numerous sorts on the market these days, some containing peat, others relying on cocoa fibre or other eco-friendly compost components. Every year I fill my greenhouse with banks of growing bags in which I raise substantial crops of beefsteak tomatoes and 'Sungold' cherry tomatoes, which are under planted with various sorts of basil. There are also one or two bags devoted to melon plants, usually 'Blenheim Sweetheart', which produce the sweetest fruits. When planting tomatoes in growing bags it is worth using a ring-culture system. This means setting the plants into a soil-filled collar that is firmed into the planting hole cut into the bag. Tomatoes will form roots where their stems come into

ABOVE: A chimney pot used as a container stand is a popular alternative use of this sort of architectural salvage.

LEFT: Growing bags are useful in greenhouse gardening and on terraces or similar situations where there is no suitable soil or free ground for crop-producing plants.

contact with water or soil. By providing extra planting depth with a compost-filled ring you make it possible for the plant to absorb greater quantities of nutrients, in turn producing heavier crops.

You can purchase stout fibre rings or else cut the bottoms out of plastic plant pots, 22.5 cm/9 in in diameter being the best size to use. Cut the openings in the bag in the usual way, put the ring in place, firming in by about 2.5 cm/1 in, but making sure it does not touch the bottom of the bag since the roots must be able to extend into the compost. Set the plant into the soil filled ring, planting it up to its first pair of leaves (do this even if you don't use the ring culture system). Water and feed regularly.

Choosing the Plants

Having detoured to the kitchen garden, let's return to the flower garden. Unlike choosing plants to suit the soil and habitat found within the garden, with a container garden you can grow whatever you like because you can generally suit the soil and growing conditions to the plants you wish to grow. The only criteria really is one of effect; what do you want the display to be like? A vibrant collection of summer-flowering annuals is the traditional approach to container gardens, but why not take the chance to grow some really exotic half-hardy plants?

BELOW: Massed groups of potted plants combine to form a wonderful containerised herbaceous border.

RIGHT: A typical country house container garden.

Petunias, ivy, trailing geraniums, impatiens, fuchsias and lobelias are standard container choices but, when there are few limits to what you can grow, it is worth stretching your creativity (and pocketbook) just that bit further to acquire plants like *Salvia grahamii*, *Briza maxima*, *Melianthus major*, *Anisodontea capensis*, *Sphaeralcea munroana* and *Mimulus auranticus*. These hardy plants will extend your display since many of them will flower brilliantly well into late summer and even to the first frost.

ABOVE: Aeoniums and agave.
BELOW: Aspidistra.
RIGHT: Summer patio

Consider also using some 'houseplants' in boxes and tubs. They are especially valuable for the strength and splendor of the their foliage and for adding a strong and dramatic structure to what might otherwise be a bitty display of tiny flowers and insignificant leaves. Among my most favourite plants for this is *Aeonium arboreum* with a rosette of broad, flat, succulent leaves.

Don't forget to treat them as you would half-hardy or tender exotics. Aspidistras have good leaves and a spell outdoors will banish any trace of dinginess; Swiss cheese plants, weeping fig, spider plant and mother-in-law's

tongue will be perfectly happy holidaying in a semi-shaded corner and will also benefit from a spell outdoors.

Glossy leafed plants like camellia and brightly tinted azaleas give good value all year round with varied foliage interest and stunning flowers, and don't forget orange and lemon trees for their heavily perfumed flowers and juicy fruit. Scented leaf geraniums and lemon verbena are also obvious choices for container gardening.

Permanent displays of dwarf evergreens and fancy ivies are a good choice for large containers; the evergreen show can be spotlighted with colourful bulbs in spring and a few annual bedding plants.

Parsley, sage, rosemary and thyme can all be grown in containers, as can most herbs. A collection nurtured near the kitchen door or else on the windowsill will brighten your day and your cooking.

Bay trees, clipped to make neat ball-shaped standards; garlic and plain chives; true French tarragon; tender annuals like basil and coriander and hardy annual herbs like dill and chervil are herbs I would never be without. Each year I make a special effort to gather the seed for next year's crop but, if I forget, which I often do, the plants take care of it, self-sowing into each other's pots – with wild abandon – and into the soil and paving cracks around the bases of the pots. In fact, this is part of a container herb

ABOVE: *Eucomis bicolor*
BELOW: **These containers link the house with garden.**

RIGHT: Hostas such as the variegated 'Francee' are magnificent foliage plants ideally suited to container growing. Position them wherever the garden needs an injection of interest.

BELOW: Herbs do well in the free-draining soil of a container and can be arranged in an attractive display making them as pretty as they are functional.

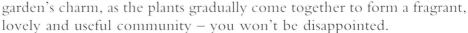

garden's charm, as the plants gradually come together to form a fragrant, lovely and useful community – you won't be disappointed.

I like mint too, but in a small garden it can take over, which is why it is a good container subject. Give it a pot of its own in the shade and be sure the pot is deep, since mint likes to delve.

Apart from mint, most herbs come from warm Mediterranean climates, so in a pot you can give them the well-drained soil and warm, sheltered position that they like. Be sure to keep the pots out of cool breezes and clip over regularly to encourage bushy growth.

There really are few restrictions on what you can grow, and the plant chapter at the back will help to give you some idea of the possibilities.

PLANTING PRACTICALITIES

HAVING CHOSEN YOUR CONTAINERS and decided on your planting theme, it is time to get busy with composts, fertilisers and the wide range of container gardening sundries available to you.

Composts

Compost is a soil substitute in which to grow plants. Like soil it provides the air, food and water required by plants, but, unlike soil, it can be specially prepared from a variety of materials so that there is a wide range of composts available.

For the purposes of container gardening, you will be most concerned with potting compost (although you may require some seed and cutting compost if you intend to raise your own plants for container growing). Potting composts are a mixture of fertiliser, materials like grit or vermiculite granules, which keep the texture open to permit good drainage, minerals, to promote plant vigour and an inorganic bulking medium of either peat, loam (soil) or coir. Peat composts give the best results, but peat is gathered from ancient bog lands around Northern Europe and is not what you could honestly call sustainable since it takes several thousand years for a peat bog to develop. However, there are approved sites and, if you buy a reputable brand, it will state this on the bag.

Coir or cocoa fibre gives good results, but loam or soil-based composts are the traditionalists choice. Recycled compost is probably the most eco-friendly you could choose and, if clean of pests and weed seed, should give good results.

If you have a place to store it, it is cheaper to buy the largest bag, generally this will be 80 litres. Peat-based compost doesn't go off and the others can have their nutrient levels topped up by adding a slow-release fertiliser, so you will always have some available since container gardens have a way of growing as new pots and plants are acquired. As a guide you should be able to fill twenty 17.5 cm/7 in pots from 80 litres. Other standard sizes are 35 litres which will fill about thirty five 17.5 cm/7in pots and 5 litres, which should take care of five or six 17.5 cm/7 in pots.

ABOVE: Good soil preparation in any container is just as important as it is in the open garden.

RIGHT: Attention to plant grooming, watering and pest and disease control is essential to achieve a good show.

Keeping the Show Going

Although the potting compost will contain fertiliser, it is only sufficient for about five to six weeks worth of growth. After that you will have to start a regime of regular feeding. However, I like to add a slow-release fertiliser to the compost. Osmacote is a good choice; this plant food compound is in a biodegradable coating that breaks down slowly each time the plant is watered, releasing the nutrients into the compost. One application of this slow-release fertiliser will feed the plants for six months.

The alternative to this is to regularly feed the plants with a water soluble fertiliser such as Phostrogen, which can be either watered into the soil or sprayed onto the leaves as a foliar feed.

Regular watering of container-grown plants is essential since pots, filled with roots and healthy, leafy top growth, will soon use up the available water. It may be necessary to do this every day to keep plants in tiptop condition. I find that watering the pots of scented geraniums, standard lemon verbenas, lilies and citrus trees, arranged on my terrace is a really relaxing and wonderfully perfumed pastime. However, it does take time to do properly since it must be done slowly, so that the water saturates rather than simply running out the bottom of the pots.

If time is a precious commodity in your life, you could try a drip irrigation system where a fine hose is run along the pots with small drip nozzles positioned on the surface of each pot. Turn on the tap and the water seeps gently into the pots.

When watering with a hose or watering can use a fine spray on the nozzle or hose since a hard stream will puddle the soil and throw up compost onto the plants. It can even rock them off their roots. If the containers are made of terracotta, stone or other porous material you should also give the outside surface a spray to keep it moist.

To maintain the appearance of the container garden you need to do rather more than feed and water regularly. As I already mentioned, the outsides of terracotta containers should be cleaned every so often to

ABOVE: Containers need frequent, thorough watering and feeding.

BELOW LEFT: A long-necked watering can is useful for hard-to-reach containers, but an extension spray attachment on a garden hose is a solution that is easier to manage.

BELOW: Garden snails often lurk in cool recessses around the rim of containers; pick them off before they damage leaves and stems.

ABOVE: A drip tube automatic watering system is the answer for low-maintenance watering.

BELOW: Topiary specimens must be kept especially tidy when container grown.

remove algae. The plants must be kept tidy and free of withered flowers and leaves. Care must also be taken to protect them against pests and diseases, on the leaves and soil borne.

Among the beasties that can do the most damage are slugs and snails; they love the cosy quarters of a moist and shady container. Tiny black slugs snuggle up just below the soil surface and snails will be found just under the rim of pots and tubs. Snails can be picked up and disposed of in your chosen fashion (my chickens love them). Slugs, however, are more problematical, especially if you have small children or pets (of any size), since there is always the danger that curiosity will goad them into nibbling a slug pellet or tasting the gel. Placing poison under half a grapefruit rind isn't really an option since it would spoil the decor of your container garden. Watered-in slug killer is probably the best bet. This is also the method to use to remove earthworms and ants that enter from the bottom of the pot through the drainage holes and create havoc with the root systems. If you notice small heaps of crumbled compost on the surface of the pot it is earthworms; piles of finely grained compost at the base or under the tub means ants.

Pests and diseases such as green fly and mildew will spread like wildfire through the humid and close quarters of a well-watered leafy container garden. An ounce of protection is worth a pound of cure, so be sure to remove any dead leaves from the plants and prune off withered growth and faded flowers to keep a clean growing environment. If that isn't enough, use a systemic insecticide and a fungicide at the very first sign of attack.

One other attribute of keeping plants free of dead material is that it will also keep the container garden looking attractive. Just as plants in the open garden benefit from dead-heading, pruning and shaping, so will the plants in pots. Annuals will bloom longer if the faded flowers are regularly removed. The same is true of herbaceous perennials, many of which will give another show if dead-headed. Withered, tattered or yellowed leaves distract from the beauty of a plant so remove these regularly. With deciduous shrubs or trees you can prune to keep a good shape and to keep the plant in proportion to its surroundings and size of container it is in.

If plants are in their final size of container it will be necessary to freshen the compost each spring by removing the top few inches of compost and replacing it with fresh compost. This is when I would add another dose of slow-release fertiliser. Spring is the start of the growing season and the time when plants, which have outgrown their containers, should be moved to the next size up. Shake some of the old compost off the roots when moving it into its new home and don't forget to feed and water regularly to be sure the plant does not receive too severe a check on its growth.

PERFECT PLANTING

NOW THAT YOU HAVE THE BASICS of container gardening at your command, it is time to do the planting. The skills involved are not all that different from planting in the open garden, but there are a few special techniques which will help you to achieve the full to overflowing look that is so appealing in container gardens.

The first principle is don't be mean; use plenty of plants and then some more. You can thin out later if necessary.

Be bold with colours. If going for a sophisticated monochrome scheme be sure to have a good contrast between the lightest light tints of one colour and its darkest darks. For vibrancy go for schemes that make use of contrasting or opposite colours: purple and orange, blue and yellow or red and green.

BELOW: This seasonal planting for spring makes use of muscari, polyanthus and hyacinths.

Window Boxes

Having made sure that the box is secure in its moorings put a thin layer of broken crocks or fine gravel in the base of the box; this is to help the drainage since waterlogged soil goes 'sour' and plants can rot.

Fill the box to within 5 cm/2 in of the top with compost. Plant up with your selected scheme, beginning in the centre and working outwards to achieve an even balance of colour and size.

Like most large containers, window boxes are left in place year-round. But because they are at a window they are more obvious and, if left ungardened during the winter, will give the facade a blank, dreary stare. For this reason it is a good idea to incorporate a few evergreens into the scheme; you can plant annuals around them during the rest of the year changing the colour display with the seasons. Dwarf evergreens with a nice fastigiate habit and trailing ivy are an obvious choice; or look for ones that have good variegation, like the dwarf, golden variegated box or a bright berry like the little Butcher's Broom (*Arctostaphylos uva-ursi)* that has lipstick-red fruits in the winter. Underplant with dwarf narcissi or species tulips.

RIGHT: Summer shows can be made up from a range of standard annuals and tender flowering plants, such as brachycome, verbena and the lovely lobelia.

Window boxes lend themselves to trailing plants; you can either plant the box entirely with such a scheme, using the expanding range of trailing pelargoniums to mimic the luxuriant displays so popular in European gardens, or use just one or two plants like *Ballota pseudodictamnus,* which has a small, rounded leaf that looks like it's cut from grey felt (there is also a yellowy-green variety). There are plenty of trailers to choose from.

Remove the plants from their pots or black plastic poly-pots and plant deeply and firm in well. Fill the box with compost to within 2.5 cm/1 in of the top and then water the plants with a fine rose fitted on the watering can or using a fine spray.

If a plant fades it should be removed rather than left in the hopes that it will recover as it will spoil the look of the box and may spread disease to the other plants. Some container gardeners make changeovers easier by working on the old-fashioned plunge system. To do this, fill the box with a loose compost and simply plunge the potted plant into it, making sure

ABOVE: Trailing plants.

RIGHT: Four pots of uniform impatiens make a single, simple design statement on a cottage windowsill, proving that sometimes less is more.

BELOW LEFT: An evergreen foliage planting of trailing ivy, shrubby skimmia and japonica gives a window box interest even in winter.

BELOW: Hanging baskets require height as well as depth in finished planting.

that the whole pot and rootball is submerged; then water in well and regularly thereafter.

Hanging Baskets

The description given here is for planting a wire-mesh hanging basket; there are no special techniques for planting the plastic bowl type of basket as it is much the same as planting a flowerpot. Because they are able to retain water, plastic is the low-maintenance choice, but wire baskets do allow you to be more adventurous.

Baskets can be suspended from overhanging eaves, the cross-beams of pergolas, from metal brackets fitted to the house wall or any architectural feature that can be fitted with a hook or bracket. When choosing where to site the basket, do keep in mind whether it will be in the way once it is suspended as you don't want to be ducking it everytime you cross the terrace but, at the same time, be sure it is accessible for watering. A word of caution here; it can be extremely dangerous climbing up and down ladders or steps with a full watering can and it is all to easy to overbalance when actually watering. It is therefore worth investing in the various fittings available that will help you to raise and lower the basket for watering. You can also purchase extension sprays for the garden hose to save the pain and possible disablement of a serious fall.

Be sure the support you have selected for the basket is up to the job; a full basket, well-watered, is a substantial and weighty object. It helps to choose a lightweight compost, one without loam in its content. There are mixes available specifically for hanging baskets and some of these have water-retaining swell-gel granules incorporated. The granules can also be purchased to add to compost. Swell-gels are no substitute for regular watering, but come in handy if you forget the task or are away from the garden for a day or two. Also, bear in mind that a larger basket will hold more compost, so choose the largest size you can. That way you will be able to grow a larger display, which will last longer because of the extra root space.

Because a basket is made from open mesh, it must be lined to contain the compost. There are various ways of doing this and the most attractive, sphagnum moss, is also the most traditional. It is available from garden centres but, like peat, it is not particularly eco-friendly to use it. There are substitutes, including a spun fibre made from coconuts and tinted green; it looks rather like the angel floss used to decorate Christmas trees. There are also mats available made from coconut or inorganic fibres, which will contain the dirt and hold a certain amount of moisture. Plastic sheeting is also used to line baskets, but never on its own.

When planting a hanging basket you begin by lining the basket with the moss or fibre matting. To hold the basket steady while you work, prop it in a bucket. Put the moss in place in thick handfuls and don't be mean.

Next, cut a circle of plastic sheeting (black or green) and slash halfway across the diameter so that it will overlap neatly to take the shape of the basket. Lay it over the moss liner, gently poke a few drainage holes through and then begin to fill the basket with compost. Incorporate any additions like slow-release fertiliser and swell-gels. Take care not to dislodge the moss as you firm the compost into the basket.

Use a tall or striking plant for the central position and then arrange the remaining plants around it. Experiment with their positions before planting them and aim to achieve a well-balanced display. Make good use of training plants by positioning them near the edges. If you have nimble fingers you can plant through the sides of the basket. Do this before you have filled the basket and planted the top. First, tease the roots of the plant through the mesh, parting the moss

ABOVE: **Summer basket.**

RIGHT: **A cottage garden.**

BELOW: **Mangers**

and gently guiding the roots through. Make a small slit in the plastic and ease the roots through, then cover them with a layer of compost. Finish planting the basket and then water well. I like to leave baskets to soak for several hours, but you must let them drain off in order to reduce the weight for positioning.

Mangers are another type of basket, usually made from narrow strips of metal welded to form a half-basket shape. They are generally fixed to walls and can double as window boxes if positioned beneath the window sill. Plant just as you would a hanging basket.

Urns, Barrels and Tubs

These tend to be the largest containers, offering a good chance to grow a wide range of plants, from small trees to tiny trailing herbs. Often these containers have an element of permanent planting; keep this in mind when deciding where to place the container so that a few years down the line you're not confronted with a tub that has to be dismantled because the contents have outgrown their position in the garden. You must also consider where you intend to position the container and if it is suitable for the plants you wish to grow – if it is in full sun, you'll be watering frequently, a task not everyone enjoys.

Remember, once a large container is planted it is virtually immovable, unless, of course, you apply the block and tackle. Alternatively, stout casters fixed to blocks of wood and attached to the base of the container will make it possible to shift it over even ground. Use three casters rather than four for steadiness.

LEFT: A *tondo* is a large terracotta tub such as those shown here, which are planted with clipped box. They are ideal for any permanent shrubby plantings.

RIGHT: A wooden tub lacks the elegance of a *tondo* but will nevertheless provide a sturdy container for a shrub or small tree such as this willow.

Be sure there are adequate drainage holes in the base of the container; wooden barrels must have the holes drilled. Cover the drainage holes, but don't block them, with a layer of broken crocks and fine gravel then fill the container with compost to within 10 cm/4 in of the top. If you are planting a tree or large shrub, only put in enough compost to raise the plant to the correct height in the container, then put the plant in place and fill with compost around its root ball, firming the compost as you go.

Strawberry pots are the sort with openings around their sides through which the plants are grown. You can use them for their designated purpose – strawberry growing – and it will keep the fruit clean and out of the reach of all but the most determined mice. You can also plant them up decoratively with a wide range of annuals and biennials, foliage plants or a collection of herbs.

You must put drainage in the bottom of the pot and use a peat or cocoa-based compost as loam composts have a tendency to wash out of the pockets during watering. Fill with compost to the first layer of openings and insert the plants, roots first, firming them into the compost. Fill with more compost to the next layer and insert more plants, always work from the outside to the inside.

RIGHT: The wooden slat construction of these containers echoes the linear form of the background trellis.

Raised Beds

These low walls of brick or stone – constructed to form planting areas around the perimeter of a terrace or against a flight of steps, or simply to elevate planting areas around a garden – are containers on a large architectural scale. More importantly, they offer wheelchair gardeners, and others with limited mobility, a chance to exercise their green fingers.

Considerations when planning for a raised bed include the height, which should be only enough to make it easy to reach for cultivation, and the width – just enough for a comfortable stretch. Allow for easy access

LEFT: Raised beds form the terrace edging and open further possibilities for gardening; they also help create a showy entrance. Here the brick paving carries into the retaining wall of an herbaceous bed planted with familiar cottage garden perennials, including foxgloves and aquilegias.

RIGHT: Raised beds, like stone sinks, help alpine gardeners to provide growing conditions demanded by their exacting plants.

LEFT: The effect created by making a raised bed behind one at ground level gives an extra dimension to the planting area.

for wheelchair-mobile gardeners by making sure the paths around and to the garden are wide enough and be sure the paving is non-slip when wet. It helps to have water easily accessible and a storage area not too far away where fertilisers, tools and so on can be stored. Also be sure to leave drainage holes around the base of the raised beds, so that water does not collect in the foundations.

Regard the raised beds as giant containers and fill the bottom with rubble and crocks. Depending on what you wish to grow you should fill by at least two-thirds, cutting down on the amount of compost you would have to use.

Over the rubble put a layer of sand or lawn turves, turned grass side down, then a layer of newspaper. Soak this subsoil well, making sure that the paper and turves (or sand) are well saturated. Then fill with good quality gardening compost using a loam-based mix for preference. You can then garden away as though it were ground level.

Raised beds can be combined with moulded pond liners to create simple water gardens by simply catching the edge of the liner in the jointing of the brick or stonework border. It is essential that the pond be level so be sure to keep excavations level. This is explained in the *Water Gardening* book in this series.

RIGHT: Acid-loving camellias get the soil conditions they need in a container. Here 'Contessa Lavinia Maggi' grows with the rampant rambling rose *Banksia lutea*.

CONTAINER GARDEN PLANTS

JUST AS WHEN PLANNING A SCHEME for the open garden, you should try to include trees and shrubs to give the collection structure, either from the evergreen specimens you include or from the character of branch, trunk and bark.

Go for slow-growing trees and shrubs that have a well-defined habit of growth. Flowering trees and shrubs will perform well and ornamentals like the cutleaf Japanese maples can be displayed to their best advantage. Exotics, plants that would not survive winter out doors in temperate climates, can be grown in containers and then moved to a frost-free shelter. Some of the exotics make excellent focal points in container garden schemes. Whatever you choose bear in mind that the mature height of the tree should be somewhere in the region of twice the diameter of the container.

Trees

Acer palmatum 'Dissectum Atropurpureum' grows to about 1 m /3 ft in a mound of feathery wine-coloured leaves.

Malus sargentii grows slowly to about 3 m/10 ft and has a graceful, spreading habit with delicate spring flowers and vivid autumn leaves.

Prunus serrulata are the Japanese ornamental cherries that give a pretty, floral display in spring and often make bright autumn leaves. 'Amanogawa' has a fastigiate habit of growth while 'Kiku-shidare zakura' is a weeping tree that would look nice in many types of containers.

Ornamental standards such as holly trees, Portuguese laurels, bay trees and box and lemon verbena can all be trained as standards to make formal displays in containers.

Train a standard by leading a single stem up a cane, tying it loosely around the cane as it gains height. Take care not to damage the tip of the stem; if it is broken off side growths will be encouraged to grow. Any side growths (laterals) that do develop should be carefully removed. When the main stem reaches the desired height, pinch out the growing tip. As the laterals develop they can be pruned back by one-third to encourage them to branch out.

ABOVE: *Acer palmatum dissectum*
RIGHT: **Conifers in pots.**
BELOW: **Bay tree,** *Laurus nobilis.*

Dracaena marginata 'Colorama' has fine, narrow leaves striped yellow and red and is often sold as a houseplant.

Lemon and orange trees have traditionally been grown in containers as they benefit from being pot-bound, so don't be in a big hurry to pot them on. Just refresh the soil every year and give a high-nitrogen feed in early spring and then a general purpose feed occasionally during the rest of the year and these trees will be happy.

ABOVE: *Acer palmatum* **and** *A. palmatum dissectum* **in large clay pots on the patio.**

EVERGREENS
Dwarf evergreens are low-maintenance, high-value trees for container gardens since their presence guarantees year-round display.

Picea abies 'Ohlendorffii' has a neat, rounded habit; short, stubby branches and a pleasing blue-grey colour.

Chamaecyparis lawsoniana 'Gnome' is the miniature relative of the common garden hedging plant. It and *C. lawsoniana* 'Minima' have rounded habits; nice additions to any container garden.

Juniperus communis 'Hibernica' makes a nice spire. It is slow-growing, especially in comparison to the other upright juniper 'Skyrocket', which does just that – avoid it for container gardens.

Cryptomeria japonica 'Elegans Compacta' has an ill-defined shape, but good purple-bronze colouring while *C. japonica* 'Spiralis' makes a spreading web of drooping branches.

Cordyline australis is a slow-growing evergreen with long, strap-like leaves. There are a number of cultivars with leaves variegated or tinged in shades of cream, yellow, pink and purple-bronze.

BELOW: Topiary in terracotta containers: box spirals and bay tree standards.

LEFT: *Lonicera nitida* standards and rhododendron decorate this terrace garden.

Shrubs

There are so many possible choices of shrubs for containers it is difficult to know where to begin when making a recommendation. Perhaps the easiest method of selection is to stick to a theme. For example, if you have a semi-shaded, woodland feel to the surroundings of your container garden, because, for instance, your garden is overshadowed by the neighbour's trees or hedge, you could grow rhododendrons and azaleas, daphnes, skimmia, winterbox, camellias and so on. All have evergreen leaves and wonderful flowers (some with a powerful perfume) and don't mind partial shade.

On the other hand if the site is in the sun all day, go for the grey-leafed Mediterranean shrubs like lavender, artemisia, cistus and so on. Exploit the sunshine even more by growing some true exotics like dwarf fan palms, cigar flowers, lantanas, abutilons or anything which catches your eye. These are just a few which have caught mine over the years.

Abutilon pictum 'Thompsonii' has variegated maple-shaped leaves splashed with a rich, egg yolk yellow and faded orange flowers. 'Kentish Belle' has the same upright, branching habit but dark green leaves and dainty red and yellow flowers.

RIGHT: **Small patio roses and miniature roses are suitable for pot growing.**

BELOW: *Pinus mugo* **in a lovely stone container.**

Berberis thunbergii 'Atropurpurea Nana' is a dwarf form of the familiar purple-leafed shrub; 'Rose Glow' is splashed with white and pale pink; 'Aurea' has gold leaves and 'Erecta' is fastigiate.

Chamerops humilis is the dwarf fan palm that produces 1 m/3 ft wide fans of shiny, green, strap-shaped leaves. A real eyecatcher, it adds a touch of splendour to simple container schemes.

Cistus albidus is half-hardy with woolly leaves and white flowers; 'Peggy Sammons' has small leaves and lovely, lavender-pink flowers; *C. corbariensis* has waxy leaves, white flowers and pink-tinged flower buds.

Convolvulus cneorum has satin, velvet-grey leaves and white 'Morning Glory' like flowers; it really glows in the garden.

Cuphea ignea is a tender plant known as the cigar flower for its bright orange, tubular flowers, which appear over a long season. It has a spreading habit and is good to mix with container plants like the lovely yellow-flowered bidens. It grows easily from cuttings taken in the late summer.

Daphne odora, D. bholua, D. cneorum 'Eximia', *D.* x *burkwoodii* 'Somerset' and *D. tangutica* are just a few of the sweetly perfumed tribe that you should grow. They are all evergreen or nearly so and have clusters of tiny, pastel-pink, tubular flowers in early spring.

Fuchsias provide the widest range of popular container plants in colours ranging from nearly white to deep burgundy; the flowers can be dainty or extravagantly double; some fuchsias are hardy while others are

ABOVE: **Azalea and japonica 'Mother's Day' in standard plastic containers.**

ABOVE: **Rosemary, pelargonium, verbena and lobelia in a tub.**

ABOVE: Ornamental maple and delicate azalea accentuate the oriental feel of the moon-gate opening in the brick wall surrounding this garden.

tender. They can be grown as shrubs, pruned and trained as standards or their natural trailing habit makes them a favourite for window boxes and hanging baskets. It is in this situation that the pendant flowers of the more showy sorts come into their own.

Fatsia japonica is often seen as a houseplant, but it also does well out of doors. It has glossy, green, broad-lobed leaves and tumbels of greenish white insignificant flowers.

Hebe 'Pagei', 'EA Bowles', 'Boughton Dome' and 'Blue Gem' are good representatives of this useful evergreen, ever-grey group of shrubs that bear wonderful flower spikes in shades of pink, purple, blue and white in early summer.

Jasminum officinale, Jasmin, is really a climber, but you can grow it twined round a tripod of canes planted in a large container. If you do this then grow something really special like *J. mesnyi* with its richly perfumed, yellow flowers and soft, evergreen foliage. I brought a snippet home from my cousin's Roman garden, rooted it in sandy compost, and it is now thriving on winters spent in the greenhouse and summers on my windswept East Anglian terrace.

Lavendula, Lavender, is usually grown as a hedge plant, but some of the pretty half-hardy species would do well in a container. These include *Lavandula stoechas,* which is 'French lavender'; *L. pedunculata* where the flower tip has wings and the lacy-leafed *L. canariensis.*

Melianthus major is an exotic foliage plant, which is rather tender except in the mildest of climates so a good subject for a container. It also has a peculiar scent that you either love or hate. I love its chocolate, burnt toast smell. It grows quite tall to about 90 cm/3 ft and has steely, blue-grey leaves with sawtooth edges.

Roses can be grown in containers but you must be sure to choose ones that are compact or low and spreading. Many of the David Austin English roses would do well in large containers as they tend to be rather lax growing. You would need several grouped together to make a good show in the garden, but in containers, they mingle easily with companions. There are also miniature or patio roses that are specially bred for small growing spaces. I would like to recommend old roses to you since these are my favourites, but container plants have to work hard and many old roses bloom only once in early summer. There are, however, repeat flowering old roses and these are worth investigating, particularly some of the old China roses like 'Hermosa', which is a shell-pink beauty bearing clusters of tea-scented, dainty flowers over a long season.

Rosmarinus officinalis is the common garden rosemary, but there are a number of varieties worth looking for including 'Severn Sea' with fine, thready leaves and blue flowers; 'Tuscan Blue' with bright blue flowers and the old-fashioned 'Gilded Rosemary' with leaves splashed yellow.

Rhododendrons and azaleas require acid soil to do well and their exacting needs can be well provided for in a container. Cultivars of *R. Yakushimanum* are especially good and have attractive foliage and tight clusters of bell-shaped flowers.

Salix hastata is a curious willow tree with upright branches covered in silver catkins like a natural bonsai tree. *S. lanata* has short, stubby stems and covered, chubby catkins amidst its lovely foliage that is quite woolly and silvery-grey.

ABOVE: Sage, thyme, chives, rosemary and purple basil in a purpose-built herb pot.

RIGHT: Pink azalea 'Beethoven'.

ABOVE: **Flowering standard lantanas decorate the entrance to this herb garden.**

Salvia officinalis is common sage but, like rosemary, there are ornamental forms to look out for including 'Purpurascens', purple-leafed sage; 'Tricolor' with pink, white and purple variegated leaves and 'Icterina' with yellow-tinged leaves. There is also a white flowered form of the common sage. Tender ornamental sages that are beneficial for container gardens include: *S. grahamii* with vivid, scarlet flowers and *S. involucrata* 'Bethelii' with clusters of shocking pink flowers at the end of upright branches (this is really more of an herbaceous perennial). A hardy ornamental good for containers is *S. blancoana*, which has whippy stems bearing bright blue flowers above the narrow, pale grey foliage. It makes a low spreading mat where the others are more upright.

Perennials

It is hard to think of a perennial which you can't grow in a container – the question is, would you want to grow it? Many perennials have great flowers for a few weeks during spring or summer, but once the flowers fade there is little left to get excited about. In a container garden you have to keep thinking 'value, value, value' and for my money this is where foliage comes into play. When perusing the catalogues and nursery stock, look first for good leaves. If there are pretty flowers as well, all the better.

Hostas offer the most delicious selection of foliage, from huge glaucous leaves with a quilted texture to tiny little sprays of shiny, variegated greenery. The choice is vast and becoming more so with more introductions

ABOVE: *Agave americana* **'Mediopicta' and** *Carex comans* **in a glazed pot.**

every year. If you intend to go for permanent planting in a collection of containers, I don't think it is worth doing unless you seek out the specials as that is what will make it really worthwhile.

Hostas come into leaf during spring and early summer, so therefore make good companions for rhododendrons. They are both woodland plants and prefer a measure of shade, although they will grow in sun. If you don't want to grow them in the same (large) container, put the hosta in its own pot. When the flowers fade and leaves begin to wither, the pot can be moved out of sight.

Hostas to look for are *H. fortunei* 'Albomarginata', 'Francee' and 'Fringe Benefit', all with varying degrees of white variegation and large leaves; 'Wide Brim', 'Dawn' and 'Shade Fanfare' with yellow variegation; 'Dorset Blue', 'Blue Angel' and 'Blue Umbrellas' are glaucous blue; 'Golden Prayers', 'Gold Standard' and 'Sum and Substance' are all a soft yellowy-green. 'Sum and Substance' has particularly large leaves.

Grasses and sedges are the optimum foliage plant and are steadily gaining in popularity as gardeners begin to appreciate the subtle colours of their leaves as they change through the seasons. Grass seedheads are also quite beautiful and an autumn display of faded brown, rust and biscuit tints is a real treat. Grasses also add movement and music as the leaves sigh and sway softly in the summer breeze.

Carex buchananii grows to 60 cm/2 ft and has good, coppery-red foliage, while *C. morrowii* 'Variegata' is low-growing to 15 cm/8 in and

RIGHT: **For added interest, containers can be dotted into border planting.**

has bright yellow and green striped leaves. *C. comans* has silvery-grey leaves and the 'Bronze Form' has much darker steely-blue leaves.

Hakonechloa macra 'Albo-Aurea' is a tall-growing, erect grass up to 45 cm/18 in tall that is boldly striped yellow.

Helictotrichon sempervirens makes a hammocky sheaf of blue foliage about 45 cm/18 in tall and carries its flower panicles well above its leaves, which gives a wonderful effect.

Miscanthus sinensis has a range of named varieties that are particularly elegant; 'Morning Light' being one of the prettiest.

But the four grasses I would grow every time are *Stipa tenuissima* – soft and flowing like silken threads and only 45 cm/18 in tall; its sister, *S. gigantea*, which sends up flower stems that nearly reach 2 m/6 ft high from

ABOVE: A balcony transformed into a beautiful garden by container-grown plants.

RIGHT: *Lilium regale* **grown in a container can be moved around to ensure that its delicious perfume is enjoyed to the fullest extent.**

LEFT: Lilies, violas and tender French lavender in a traditional jardiniere-style container.

mock of dusty-green foliage. Its seedheads are fantastically pretty, bobbing and glittering in the breeze.

The other two are brightly coloured. *Milium effusum* 'Aureum', also known as 'Bowles' Golden Grass', does best in shade where the bright yellow leaves and feathery seedheads light up the shadows. It also seeds readily, which is always nice. Finally, I'd make room for *Uncinia* N *rubra*, which has good mahogany-red, glossy leaves. It only grows to 30 cm/12 in and I have filled two formal urns with it; the rusty-red goes well with the lichen and moss patching the stonework.

Euphorbias, especially the slightly tender *E.* x *martinii*, epimediums, in all their variety, ferns, pulmonarias, bronze and green fennel and cardoons are just a fraction of the good perennial foliage to experiment with; changing the pots and the display as the seasons and your skills as a plants-person progress.

Bulbs and corms fit in with perennials, and in containers you can grow some weird and wonderful things like *Eucomis bicolor*, known as the 'pineapple plant' because of the shape of the flower spike. Lilies are also good in pots because they get the drainage they like. I suggest going for *Lilium auratum*, the golden-rayed lily of Japan or else the 'Madonna Lily', *L. candidum*, a favourite in cottage gardens. This species likes to bake in dry conditions so a pot would serve it nicely.

Dwarf narcissus can be worked into permanent container schemes and left to increase slowly. 'Jumblie', 'Hawera' and 'Jack Snipe' are just a few of the delightful spring flowers to scatter beneath a flowering shrub. *Iris reticulata*, hardy cyclamen or 'Snowdrops' could all be included to herald winter's end in the container garden.

RIGHT: Group display of annuals and perennials in terracotta pots.

BELOW: Hedera made into interesting topiary shapes by training around the stems.

Annuals and Biennials

Having encouraged you to be bold and adventurous with trees, shrubs and perennials – the permanent members of the container cast – I feel that this group of plants offers the opportunity for some instant gardening.

Once upon a time, the annuals and biennials you could buy from the nurseries, market stall-holders and garden centres was severely limited. But the trade has come a long way in the past few years and we are now able to purchase an enormous range of bedding plants in a huge range of colours to suit just about any scheme you could dream up. Of course, seed sowing may be a passion, but since annuals are disposable I can't see the point of spending all that time pricking out, hardening off and planting out, when I can go straight into business with a pre-pack of colour-schemed annuals. They are the rent-a-crowd filling; the stage around the main players. You can even purchase pre-selected annuals colour-schemed into hanging basket collections. But maybe that is taking it just a bit too easy.

Annuals and biennials are traditionally purchased in trays, usually made of white expanded polystyrene. These can be purchased in entirety or,

ABOVE: **Even the least promising space, such as this narrow stone access area, can become a garden with a collection of container-grown annuals, shrubs and perennials.**

60

ABOVE: Annuals for container gardening can be obtained from nurseries and garden centres.

alternatively, strips can be broken off to give you fewer plants. A wide range of annuals are now available as baby plants, an intermediate size between seedling and the standard size sold in trays. These little 'plug's plants' grow away quite happily as they will not have the competition tray-grown annuals experience, vying with each other in close quarters for nutrients and water.

You should look for plants that have healthy foliage without any trace of wilting or yellowing, which indicates a stressed out plant; it will never recover. The plants should not be leggy or drawn looking. This is known as etiolated and is an indication that the plant has not had enough light after germination. Don't automatically choose a tray that is covered with the most flowers; this can also indicate stress as the plant struggles to make seed before dying. The best way to get annuals and biennials is when they are young and robust so that they will root readily into their new container home.

If you want to be a more hands-on type of gardener, then you can purchase pots of germinated seedlings, which allows you to prick them out into the trays provided and grow them until it is time to plant out. If you are a novice gardener or are not able to provide the correct type of conditions for germinating trays and pots of seeds (even warmth and low light), then these seedling packs are a boon.

Don't forget that you must not put tender plants out into the garden until all danger of frost is past.

There are bedding and trailing annuals and biennials; the former have an upright, bushy habit, while the latter explains itself and can be used at the front of container displays or else tickled through the larger growing shrubs and perennials to weave a fanciful tapestry of flower colour.

BELOW: Planting a terracotta trough raised to be within easy reach allows for better access when gardening.

WHITE BEDDING
Alyssum 'Snowdrift'
Lobelia 'Whitelady'
Impatiens 'Accent White'
Geranium 'Century White'
Petunia 'Express White'
Chrysanthemum frutescens 'Double White'

WHITE TRAILING
Fuchsia 'Harry Gray'
Verbena 'White Cleopatra'
Petunia 'Cascadia White'

PINK/RED BEDDING
Fuchsia 'Pink Spangles'
Geranium 'Apple Blossom'
          'Multibloom Red'
Chrysanthemum 'Breitner Rose'

Chrysanthemum frutescens 'Pink Dwarf'
Pansy 'Red Wing'
        'Rose Blotch'
Impatiens 'Rose Star'
Petunia 'Pink Morn'
        'Crimson Star'

PINK/RED TRAILING
Fuchsia 'Eva Boerg'
        'Pink Galore'
        'Cascade'

Verbena 'Sissinghurst Pink'
        'Red Cascade'
Lotus berthelotii
Polygonum 'Pink Bubbles'
Lobelia 'Red Cascade'
Ivy leaf geranium 'Sugar Baby'
                'Super Rose'

BLUE/PURPLE BEDDING
Ageratum 'Blue Mink'
Lobelia 'Cambridge Blue'
        'Crystal Palace'
Petunia 'Light Blue'
Geranium 'Multibloom Lavender'
Impatiens 'Accent Violet'
        'Accent Lavender Blue'
Brachyscome 'Break O' Day'

BLUE/PURPLE TRAILING
Fuchsia 'Stanley Cash'
Lobelia 'Lilac Fountain'
        'Blue Cascade'
Verbena 'Blue Cascade'

YELLOW/ORANGE TRAILING
Ivy 'Golden Child'
Bidens

YELLOW/ORANGE BEDDING
Tagetes 'Golden Gem'
Marigold 'African Perfection
        Orange'

ABOVE: A lavishly planted, wall-mounted container with hebe, fuchsia, petunia, pelargonium, lobelia, verbena and helichrysum.

ABOVE: Use your imagination – even the most esoteric object can be a container gardener's dream come true.

This is only a small sample of the range of annuals and biennials available; there are also primulas for spring displays as well as forget-me-nots, extravagant dahlias, subtle foliage plants like helichrysum and pansies in every shade of the rainbow. It is quite overwhelming really.

INDEX

(References to photographs are indicated by *italics*.)

1

63

Picture Acknowledgements
The work of the following photographers has been used:
David Askham: 51, 61(b), 62(t); John Baker: 52; Jon Bouchier:
32(b); Lynne Brotchie: 9, 12(t), 20, 25(b), 30, 31, 34(t), 37, 43,
44(b), 53, 62(b); Linda Burgess: 6; Tommy Candler: 50(b);
Brian Carter: 12(c), 14(b), 29(t), 34(b); Bob Challinor: 16, 39;
Henk Dijkman: 45; Ron Evans: 23; Vaughn Fleming: 55; Nigel
Francis: 35, 60; John Glover: i, 8, 11, 18(t), 25(t), 27, 33(b),
58(b); Marijke Heuff: 24(t); Neil Holmes: 17; John Hooton:
15(b); Michael Howes: 18(b), 26, 33(t), 50(t); Lamontagne:
14(t), 29(b), 32(t), 38 and jacket; Jane Legate: 19; Zara
Mccalmont: 28(t); John Neubauer: 15(t); Jerry Pavia: 24(b), 40,
54, 55(t); Joanne Pavia: 59; Howard Rice: 44(t); JS Sira: 28(b),
41, 48(b); Ron Sutherland: 13(t), 28(bl), 42, 47, 48(t), 56;
Brigitte Thomas: 22(b); Mel Watson: 57, 61(t)Steven Wooster:
ii, 7, 10, 12(b), 13(b), 21, 22(t), 36, 46, 49, 58(t).

The following designers worked on some of the photographed
material:
Andrea Parsons Design: 42; Anthony Noel Garden/Design,
Fulham: 12(b), 13(b), 36, 58(t); Anthony Paul: 46; Cathy
Boardman & Serena Blackie Design: 10; Duane Paul Design
Team: 7; Michele Osborne Design: 13(t), 47, 48(t).

The following gardens were photographed:
Admington Hall, Warwickshire, England: 16; Four Acres,
Surrey, England: 21; Fulham Park Gardens, England: 58(t);
Harmony Garden, Help the Aged, Chelsea Flower Show 1994,
England: 42; John Zerning's balcony: 56; Joydene, Shropshire,
England: 23; Lackham College, England: 51; Littlebrook,
England: 27; Lynne Brotchie's garden, Wimbledon, England:
25(b); Martin Summers Garden, England: ii; Mien ruys garden,
Holland: 24(t); National Herb Garden, Washington D.C., USA:
54; Turn end, Buckinghamshire, England: 41; Wimbledon
Garden - D. Eadie, England: 43.